WordSTUDY VOCABULARY · Start 1

Overview & Assessment HANDBOOK

BENCHMARK EDUCATION COMPANY

Benchmark Education Company
145 Huguenot Street • New Rochelle, NY 10801

ISBN: 978-1-935473-88-6

For ordering information call **Toll-Free 1-877-236-2465** or visit our Web site at **www.benchmarkeducation.com**.

Table of Contents

Word Study & Vocabulary Assessment Tools

Appendix

Introduction

Word Study & Vocabulary Skill Bags are designed for use in comprehensive literacy and reading/writing workshop classrooms. They provide a research-based, explicit, and systematic approach to teaching the phonics, spelling, and vocabulary skills students need when reading advanced and challenging texts.

"Although children's word knowledge is enhanced by their reading and writing experiences, teacher-guided instruction and practice facilitate students' detection of patterns in words and help them internalize their understandings."

—Kathy Ganske

Welcome to Benchmark Education's Word Study & Vocabulary Skill Bags

Thank you for selecting Word Study & Vocabulary Skill Bags from Benchmark Education Company. There are four developmentally sequenced word study and vocabulary kits. The levels range from the beginning syllables and affixes stage to advanced derivational constancy stages of the developmental spelling continuum. Each skill bag kit provides all the lesson resources and tools needed for small-group instruction, guided practice, and independent practice opportunities in a classroom or intervention setting. Teachers and students alike will find the lessons and materials engaging, hands-on, and motivating.

Why Teach Word Study and Vocabulary Explicitly?

A good reader is like a builder who is able to reach into a box of familiar tools and pull out the right one at the right moment. Like tools, each reading skill or strategy has an important use in the complex cognitive process of decoding and comprehending text.

The demands of complex text and vocabulary pose challenges for students. A student who is advancing as a reader must be able to categorize, integrate, compare, and analyze graphophonic information. Without this decoding process, the student cannot move quickly to reading for meaning. Engaging students in word study gives them strategies for analyzing multisyllabic words and a deeper understanding of prefixes, suffixes, and root words. Explicit instruction in word-solving strategies helps students read and spell quickly and accurately. It also encourages comprehension.

What Are the Goals of Word Study & Vocabulary Skill Bags?

To shape the development of phonics, spelling, and vocabulary knowledge, Word Study & Vocabulary Skill Bags provide students at different stages of literacy growth with varied experiences that promote automatic and flexible control of advanced decoding and word analysis strategies. The systematic lessons will:

- Build a foundation for successful word study instruction
- Explicitly teach new and challenging word study elements
- Foster word play to support vocabulary development
- Support and motivate all learners
- Help all students achieve their full potential

What Is the Research Behind Word Study & Vocabulary Skill Bags?

Benchmark Education's Phonics Skill Bags and Word Study & Vocabulary Skill Bags support the various stages of phonics and spelling development. The continuum of development (Ganske, Bear, et al.) provides the instructional scope and sequence for the Phonics Skills Bags and for the Word Study & Vocabulary Skill Bags for Grades K–6.

Stage of Development	Characteristics	Benchmark Education Phonics Skill Bags and Word Study & Vocabulary Skill Bags
Preliterate/ Emergent	Scribbles Letter-like symbols Random letters Using letters of name Strings of letters	StartUp Phonics Skill Bags (Red Lessons)
Letter Name (Alphabetic)	Sound-by-sound word spelling and decoding Limited sight vocabulary Initial and final consonants, initial and final consonant blends, digraphs, short vowels, affricates	StartUp Phonics Skill Bags (Purple Lessons) BuildUp Phonics Skill Bags
Within Word Pattern	Reading and writing chunk parts of words VCe patterns, r-controlled vowel patterns, long vowel patterns, abstract vowels	BuildUp Phonics Skill Bags
Syllable Juncture (Syllable & Affixes)	Vowel patterns in single syllable words used correctly, learning to apply pattern knowledge within syllables and across boundaries Accented and unaccented syllable patterns, doubling, e-drop, and no spelling change, common prefixes and suffixes	SpiralUp Phonics Skill Bags Word Study & Vocabulary Skill Bags 1 (Start) Word Study & Vocabulary Skill Bags 2 (Build)
Derivational Constancy (Derivational Relations)	Morphemic analysis Silent and sounded consonants, consonant and vowel changes, Greek and Latin elements, assimilated prefixes	Word Study & Vocabulary Skill Bags 3 (Spiral) Word Study & Vocabulary Skill Bags 4 (Extend)

" . . . word study encompasses phonics, spelling, and vocabulary instruction, with children's orthographic or spelling knowledge of central importance in determining timely instruction with word sorting as a key activity. As children move into more sophisticated word studies, spelling and vocabulary development receive increasing attention."

—Kathy Ganske

Benchmark Education's Word Study & Vocabulary Skill Bags include the following elements of effective instruction to support advanced word analysis and vocabulary development.

- **Assessments that inform instruction**

- **Modeled, guided, and independent practice**

- **Whole-group, small-group, partner, and individual grouping configurations**

- **Linked phonics, spelling, and vocabulary development**

- **Ongoing spiraled review of previously taught skills and strategies**

- **Anchor posters, lists, and charts**

- **Short passages for connected text reading**

- **Word sorts for sound, spelling, and meaning patterns**

- **A variety of open, closed, sound, pattern, blind, written, and speed sorts**

- **Word hunts, cloze activities, and games**

- **Word study notebooks**

- **Blending and decoding practice**

- **Spelling practice and dictation**

- **Oral discussions and written reflections**

- **Home/school connections**

- **Support for English learners**

- **Word study investigations**

Like StartUp, BuildUp, and SpiralUp Phonics, the Word Study & Vocabulary Skill Bags reflect the most current research on how to teach word study effectively.

What the Research Says About Phonics, Spelling, and Vocabulary Word Study	Word Study & Vocabulary Skill Bags
"By categorizing words according to their features, students are able to notice similarities and differences within and across the categories that help them to form generalizations about how the words work." —K. Ganske, 2008	Each unit includes multisyllabic words with related patterns for comparing and analyzing.
"Once children grasp the alphabetic principle and learn the most common sound-spellings they meet in primary grade texts, their next hurdle involves decoding multisyllabic words. Explicit instruction in the six common spelling patterns, the most common syllable types, prefixes, suffixes, roots, and word origins helps students recognize larger word chunks, which makes decoding and figuring out meaning easier." —W. Blevins, 2001	The scope and sequence supports the advanced understandings of syllable juncture and derivational constancy development.
"Word study is active, and by making judgments about words and sorting words according to similar features, students construct their own understandings about how features work. Active, thoughtful practice helps students internalize word features and become automatic in using what they have learned." —D. R. Bear, M. Invernizzi, S. Templeton, F. Johnston, 2008	Each unit includes a variety of model-guide-apply learning opportunities. Word sorts, investigations, cloze passages, and interactive learning can be found in each lesson.
"Effective vocabulary instruction includes providing rich and varied language experiences, teaching individual words, teaching word learning strategies, fostering word consciousness." —M. Graves, 2006	Within every skill bag, students examine word categories and apply word solving and word analysis skills.
"English is one of the most morphologically complex languages. For every word we know, there are six or seven other words we can attach meaning to if we are 'morphologically sophisticated.'" —P. Cunningham	Students focus on units of meaning in words as they analyze Greek and Latin word elements and focus on prefixes and suffixes that alter the meanings of base words.
"As students work with words, they not only examine the sound, pattern, and meaning relationships of their spellings but also come to understand and use the words." —K. Ganske, 2008	Sorting by sound, pattern, and meaning provide support for developing multiple strategies for word learning.
"Word solving is basic to the complex act of reading. When readers can employ a flexible range of strategies for solving words rapidly and efficiently, attention is freed for comprehension. Word solving is fundamental to fluent, phrased reading." —I. Fountas & G. S. Pinnell, 2007	The systematic, explicit instruction in every skill bag promotes rapid, fluent decoding of multisyllabic words to support text comprehension.

What Are the Features and Benefits of Word Study & Vocabulary Skill Bags?

Like the Phonics Skill Bags (StartUp, BuildUp, and SpiralUp), the Word Study & Vocabulary Skill Bags build the necessary foundation for reading longer and more complex text. Following is a list of the program's benefits to students.

Features	Benefits to Students
Direct, explicit instruction in basic syllable patterns	Students learn advanced multisyllabic word-solving strategies.
Direct, explicit word study instruction	Students learn to utilize structural analysis components such as prefixes, suffixes, and root words. Word study investigation lessons spotlight additional word awareness categories and origins.
Direct, explicit spelling instruction	Students master advanced multisyllabic patterns to facilitate reading connected text.
Word sorts	Students use a variety of activities to sort and to make generalizations about words according to related patterns.
Text passages	Each unit includes a text passage for word hunt investigation activities that connect word study to reading.
Hands-on, multisensory tools	All types of learners are supported by instruction that is concrete, motivating, and multimodal.

The program also offers many benefits to the implementation site.

Features	Benefits to Site
Systematic and research based	Teachers implement best practices as they sequentially introduce skills designed for advanced phonics and word study development.
Organized, consistently formatted units and materials	Teachers at all experience levels can confidently manage the classroom and teach advanced phonics and word study with a minimum of advance preparation.
Whole-group, small-group, partner, and independent activities for every skill	Teachers have reteaching strategies and extension opportunities at their fingertips.
English learner support	Teachers can offer additional assistance in each skill to English learners.
Spiraled curriculum	Teachers continuously review prior units and build instruction on previously taught skills.
Overview & Assessment Handbook	Teachers get ongoing support, answers to important questions, and assessments to inform instruction.
Family participation	Parents can support their children's word study development utilizing the Home Connections activities.

Components at a Glance

Each of the four Word Study & Vocabulary Kits includes 32 developmentally-sequenced skill bags. Each Skill Bag includes a consistent set of teacher and student components.

Teacher's Guide

- 1 Per Skill Bag
  (8 pages each, 8 ½'' x 11'')

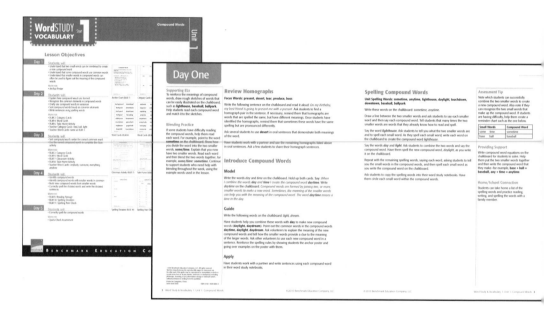

Reproducible Tools, Activities & Home Connections

- 1 Per Skill Bag (12 pages each, 8 ½" x 11")

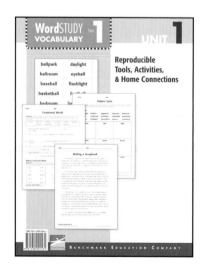

Anchor Charts

• 1 Per Skill Bag (17" x 22")

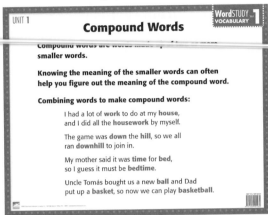

Word and Category Card Sheets

• 3 Word Card Sheets (6 copies of each sheet)

• 1 Word Sort Category Card Sheet

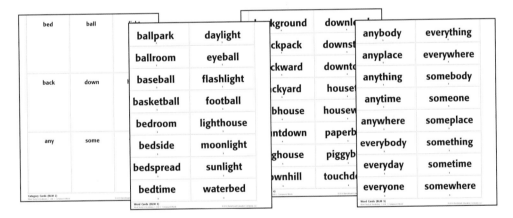

Overview & Assessment Handbook

• 1 Per Kit (64 pages)

Getting Started Checklist

Use the following checklist to help you get ready to administer assessments and prepare for instruction.

☐ **Familiarize yourself with how the program works** by reading Using the Components on pages 13–16 and reviewing the Scope and Sequence found on page 18.

☐ **Examine the Skill Bag components** and study the Teacher's Guides and reproducible blackline master booklet.

☐ **Examine the assessment tasks** on pages 20–62. Familiarize yourself with the instructions for administering, scoring, and interpreting results. See page 19: Using Assessment Results to Inform Instruction.

☐ **Administer the initial screening tasks.** Analyze the results to determine each student's starting point in the Word Study & Vocabulary Skill Bag Kits and how to group students for small-group instruction.

☐ **Review the Managing Instruction in the Phonics/Word Study Block section** found on page 17 to familiarize yourself with scheduling, pacing, and grouping for proper implementation.

Using the Components

Overview & Assessment Handbook

The Overview & Assessment Handbook contains initial screeners as well as pre- and post-assessments to determine students' strengths and needs.

This handbook provides a variety of methods to gather, record, and evaluate information about your students' phonics, spelling, and vocabulary knowledge. Based on this information, you can decide what skill instruction your students need and whether they would benefit from additional small-group or individual instruction.

Initial Screeners

Initial screeners help identify and target student needs as well as placement for intervention lessons. Student recording forms and explicit directions for administering, scoring, and analyzing results are provided for the teacher.

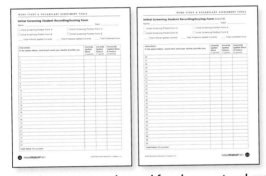

Initial screeners can be used for placement and grouping decisions.

Pre- and Post-Assessments

Use the pre- and post-assessments to evaluate a related cluster of skills within the kit. Student recording forms and explicit directions for administering, scoring, and analyzing results are provided for the teacher.

Pre- and post-assessments identify student understandings of a variety of specific features that form the targeted instructional focus of each unit.

"The most effective instruction in phonics, spelling, and vocabulary links word study to the texts being read, provides a systematic scope and sequence of word level skills, and provides multiple opportunities for hands-on practice and application."

—Bear, Invernizzi, Templeton, & Johnston

Teacher's Guides

Explicit Instruction

The 32 units in each Word Study & Vocabulary Kit teach syllable patterns, structural analysis, and vocabulary in a systematic sequence that supports current research on best practices. Each Teacher's Guide follows a consistent sequence with five days of instruction targeting one element of word study. Teachers follow the research-based, model-guide-apply instructional pattern as students review, sort, categorize, analyze, spell, read, write, and apply word-solving strategies. The cover of each unit is a visual guide to the materials needed for each day of instruction.

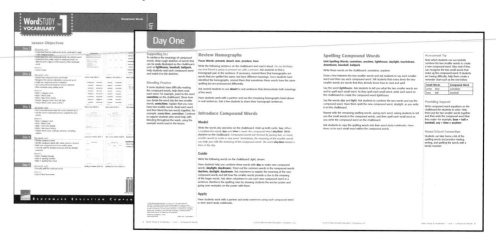

Five days of explicit instruction per Skill Bag

Quick-Check Assessments

Each Teacher's Guide contains a Quick-Check Assessment for the unit. Use this progress-monitoring tool to determine a student's need for enrichment or intervention. As you analyze student responses, note which skills or words give students difficulty, then provide further practice by using the recommended activities in each unit.

Unit Quick-Check Assessment for progress monitoring

Informal Observation

Use informal observations to note whether students are mastering the skills. If you are uncertain about a student's confidence with a particular skill, call on that student to perform the task during the lesson and observe what he or she does. If you feel the student requires more practice, use the suggested mini-lessons provided for each unit. Throughout the unit, teacher assessment tips are provided to help you make observations about student progress. Analyze students' writing samples for evidence of transfer to independent writing and for tangible evidence of spelling and vocabulary development.

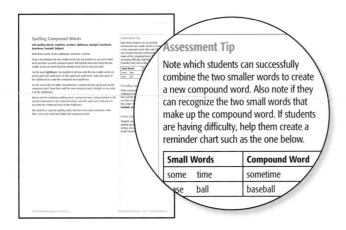

Assessment Tip

Note which students can successfully combine the two smaller words to create a new compound word. Also note if they can recognize the two small words that make up the compound word. If students are having difficulty, help them create a reminder chart such as the one below.

Small Words		Compound Word
some	time	sometime
base	ball	baseball

Reproducible Tools, Activities & Home Connections

Every unit has a corresponding blackline master booklet that includes all the reproducible tools and activities needed for instruction. A Home Connection activity for students to complete with their families is included with each unit.

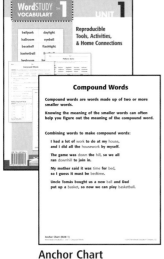

| **Anchor Chart** | **Word Card Sheets** | **Classroom Activity** | **Home Connection Activity** | **Reading Passage** |

Support Tools

High-quality, durable, and motivating manipulatives are provided to support instruction.

Anchor Poster Chart

One laminated anchor poster is provided for each unit. The words on the poster introduce the targeted word study element.

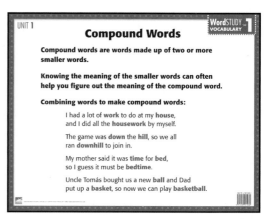

Word Cards

Three different sheets of lesson-specific word cards accompany each Skill Bag. Six copies of each sheet are provided and can be used for teacher modeling or for small-group and partner sorts and activities.

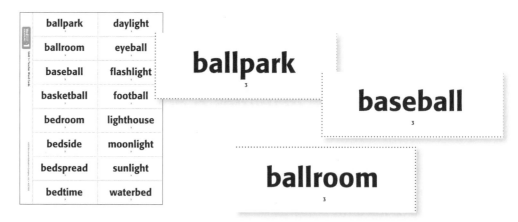

Word Sort Category Cards

One lesson-specific word sort category card sheet is included in each unit. This can be used on any surface where word sorting may occur.

Managing Instruction in the Phonics/Word Study Block

Flexible Use for Tiered Instruction

Word Study & Vocabulary Skill Bags can be used in a variety of instructional settings to provide targeted instruction for whole-group, small-group, or intervention lessons. The following chart includes options for Tier One, Two, and Three instruction.

Instructional Setting	Recommendations for Use
Tier One Core Instruction	Daily whole-group lessons to support the 30-minute phonics/word study block. Teachers begin with the first lesson and follow the scope and sequence for the entire kit. Pre- and Post-Assessments for Feature Analysis help pinpoint specific needs and support differentiating word study instruction. Partner and independent activities for each unit provide meaningful learning for individual students who have not mastered the targeted skills.
Tier Two and Three Interventions	Daily 30-minute small-group intervention lessons. Using the results from the Initial Screening Assessment, students are placed into the kit at the appropriate developmental stage to meet their individual needs. Use the Initial Screening and Placement Assessment Forms A and B on pages 25–28 to identify the kit and specific lesson for placement.

Scheduling and Pacing

Each kit contains 32 Skill Bags, enough for an entire year of instruction. Each Skill Bag is designed for five days of instruction, 20–30 minutes per day. This lesson design provides explicit instruction that matches daily core and intervention time allocations. Use some or all of the activities, depending on the needs of your students. If you want students to work more quickly and learn a new element every three days, you can select just those activities that will benefit your students the most.

Promoting Word Awareness, Consciousness, and Word Play

Each unit includes suggestions for independent practice that promote word awareness and word play. Students engage in games and hands-on investigations to extend word-solving strategies and build vocabulary. Each kit has word study investigation lessons that spotlight a variety of words such as homographs, homophones, palindromes, portmanteau words, foreign words and phrases, and more.

Scope and Sequence

Word Study & Vocabulary Scope and Sequence—Kit 1

Compound Words	
Unit 1	Compound words
Inflectional Endings	
Unit 2	Adding -ing to words with VC and VCC patterns
Unit 3	Adding -ing to words with VCe and VCC patterns
Unit 4	Review of double, e-drop, and nothing
Unit 5	Adding -ed to words
Unit 6	Unusual past tense words
Unit 7	Plural endings: adding -es, -ies
Unit 8	Irregular plurals
Unit 9	y + inflectional endings
Open and Closed Syllables	
Unit 10	Syllable juncture in VCV and VCCV patterns
Unit 11	More syllable juncture in VCV and VCCV patterns
Unit 12	Syllable juncture in VCV and VVCV patterns
Unit 13	Syllable juncture in VCCCV and VV patterns
Unit 14	Open and closed syllables and inflected endings
Vowel Patterns in Accented/Stressed Syllables	
Unit 15	Long a patterns in accented syllables
Unit 16	Long i patterns in accented syllables
Unit 17	Long o patterns in accented syllables
Unit 18	Long u patterns in accented syllables
Unit 19	Long e patterns in accented syllables
Unaccented Syllables	
Unit 20	Unaccented final syllables (le)
Unit 21	Unaccented final syllables (le, el, il, al)
Unit 22	Unaccented final syllables (er, ar, or)
Unit 23	Agents
Unit 24	Final -y, -ey, and -ie
Consonants	
Unit 25	Hard and soft c
Unit 26	Hard and soft g
Unit 27	The sound of k spelled ck, ic, and x
Affixes	
Unit 28	Prefixes (re-, un-)
Unit 29	Prefixes (dis-, mis-, pre-)
Unit 30	Suffixes (-y, -ly, -ily)
Unit 31	Comparatives (-er, -est)
Word Study Investigations	
Unit 32	Anagrams

18 WordStudy**VOCABULARY** Start 1   ©2010 Benchmark Education Company, LLC

Word Study & Vocabulary Assessment Tools

A variety of assessment tools are provided for initial screening and placement; for analysis of student strengths and needs; and for progress monitoring. The following chart provides recommendations for administering the assessments.

Assessments	Purpose	Frequency
Initial Screening Assessments	Identify students' stages of spelling development	Beginning, middle, and end of the year (3 times a year)
Pre- and Post-Feature Analysis Assessments	Identify specific understandings of each word study element for a cluster of related skills/units	Before and after a variety of units with related features (8 times a year)
Unit Quick-Check Assessments	Identify mastery or areas where additional support is needed after a week of instruction	Weekly after completing each unit

Using Assessment Results to Inform Instruction

Use the results from the Initial Screening Assessment to determine where in the Word Study & Vocabulary Skill Bags you will begin instruction. These results highlight specific areas of need for each student. They can also be used to determine placement for intervention lessons and to identify specific needs for differentiation in Tier One core instruction. See the Initial Screening and Placement Assessment Forms A and B (pages 25–28).

Storing and Managing Assessments

Create a Word Study & Vocabulary Assessment folder for each student. Collect and store the students' Initial Screener and Pre- and Post-Assessments for Feature Analysis in the folders throughout the year. These assessments provide snapshots of each student's understanding and growth over time. Store the Word Study & Vocabulary Assessment folders with student portfolios and other records. Unit Quick-Check Assessments can be sent home or stored in each student's folder.

Initial Screening and Placement Assessments

Instructions for Administering, Scoring, and Reporting Results

Administer the Initial Screening and Placement Assessments

1. Make a copy of the student recording form (page 22).

2. Administer the initial screening assessments to small groups of students at the same time or to your entire class. Note: Use the same word list for pre- and post-assessments. All students should begin with Form A. Based on their results, some students will continue the assessment using Form B.

3. Explain to students that you will be calling out words one at a time and using each word in a sentence. Students are to write each word on their recording forms.

4. Collect students' recording forms after conducting the assessment.

Score the Initial Screening and Placement Assessments (The maximum score is 100 points, 2 points per word.)

1. If the entire word is spelled correctly, score it as 2 points.

2. If the word is misspelled but the feature is spelled correctly, score it as 1 point. (See underlined features of each word on the master word lists found on pages 25–28).

3. If the word and the feature are misspelled, score it as 0 points.

4. Document any errors (misspelled words and/or features).

5. Total the score for the assessment. Record the total score at the bottom of the page.

Analyze Results and Plan for Instruction

1. Analyze the results to determine each student's level of understanding and/or appropriate placement for intervention lessons.

2. Refer to the "If" and "Then" columns on the Initial Screening and Placement Assessment Forms A and B to find the units in the Word Study & Vocabulary Skill Bags that are recommended for intervention lessons.

3. Look for evidence of transfer in students' reading and writing for application of word study and vocabulary learning.

Student Score	Recommendations
90–100%	Administer Initial Screening and Placement Assessment Form B. Recommended placement in Kits 3 or 4.
70–89%	Develop differentiated instruction and provide additional supports as needed during lessons. Recommended placement in Kits 1 or 2.
Below 70%	Provide additional supports and intervention lessons to meet student needs. Note: For additional intervention lessons for students scoring below 70%, see also the Quick Phonics Assessment and Phonics Skill Bags from Benchmark Education.

Report Results from the Initial Screening and Placement Assessments

1. Use the Initial Screening and Placement Class Summary Recording Form (page 24) to document learning over time. This form provides a summary of ongoing progress for the class throughout the school year.

2. Use the summary to flexibly group students for appropriate continued learning and intervention.

3. Color code student scores to identify small groups for additional support and intervention.

   • For students who need moderate support, highlight their scores in yellow.

   • For students who need intensive interventions and support, highlight their scores in pink (or red).

Initial Screening Student Recording/Scoring Form

Name: _____ Date: _____

☐ Initial Screening Pretest Form A   ☐ Initial Screening Posttest Form A

☐ Initial Screening Pretest Form B   ☐ Initial Screening Posttest Form B

_____ Total # Words Spelled Correctly   _____ Total # Features Spelled Correctly   _____ Total Combined Score

Instructions: In the spaces below, record each word your teacher provides you.	Correctly Spelled Word (2 points)	Correctly Spelled Feature (1 point)	Incorrectly Spelled Word & Feature (0 points)
1.			
2.			
3.			
4.			
5.			
6.			
7.			
8.			
9.			
10.			
11.			
12.			
13.			
14.			
15.			
16.			
17.			
18.			
19.			
20.			
21.			
22.			
23.			
24.			
25.			
26.			

Initial Screening Student Recording/Scoring Form *(cont'd)*

Name: _____   Date: _____

☐ Initial Screening Pretest Form A   ☐ Initial Screening Posttest Form A

☐ Initial Screening Pretest Form B   ☐ Initial Screening Posttest Form B

_____ Total # Words Spelled Correctly   _____ Total # Features Spelled Correctly   _____ Total Combined Score

Instructions: In the spaces below, record each word your teacher provides you.	Correctly Spelled Word (2 points)	Correctly Spelled Feature (1 point)	Incorrectly Spelled Word & Feature (0 points)
27.			
28.			
29.			
30.			
31.			
32.			
33.			
34.			
35.			
36.			
37.			
38.			
39.			
40.			
41.			
42.			
43.			
44.			
45.			
46.			
47.			
48.			
49.			
50.			
Total Points (100 possible)			

Initial Screening and Placement Class Summary Recording Form

Teacher Name: _____ Grade Level: _____

Student Names	Form A Pretest Date Administered:	Form A Posttest Date Administered:	Form B Pretest Date Administered:	Form B Posttest Date Administered:

Initial Screening and Placement Assessment Form A

Word	Feature	If students answer...	Then provide instruction using...
1. passport	Compound Words	1 or both items incorrectly	Word Study & Vocabulary Kit 1, Unit 1
2. one-sided			Word Study & Vocabulary Kit 2, Unit 1
3. swimming	Inflectional Endings	1 or more items incorrectly	Word Study & Vocabulary Kit 1, Units 2–9
4. riding			
5. netted			
6. nosier			
7. halves			
8. grimmest			Word Study & Vocabulary Kit 2, Units 2–3
9. bison	Open and Closed Syllables	1 or more items incorrectly	Word Study & Vocabulary Kit 1, Units 10–14
10. demand			
11. baggage			
12. fiber			
13. minnow			
14. crayon	Vowel Patterns in Accented/ Stressed Syllables	2 or more items incorrectly	Word Study & Vocabulary Kit 1, Units 15–19
15. miser			
16. molten			
17. humor			
18. dreadful			Word Study & Vocabulary Kit 2, Units 4–15
19. system			
20. nostril			
21. publish			
22. voyage			
23. rural			
24. charcoal			
25. mortal			
26. merit			

Initial Screening and Placement Assessment Form A *(cont'd)*

27. fum<u>ble</u> 28. mor<u>sel</u> 29. rum<u>or</u> 30. foun<u>der</u>	Unaccented Syllables	1 or more items incorrectly	Word Study & Vocabulary Kit 1, Units 20–24
31. fai<u>lure</u> 32. urch<u>in</u> 33. triv<u>et</u> 34. ag<u>ai</u>nst 35. obe<u>yed</u>	Unaccented Syllables	1 or more items incorrectly	Word Study & Vocabulary Kit 2, Units 16–20
36. <u>c</u>ensus 37. <u>g</u>allery 38. a<u>c</u>ademic	Consonants	1 or more items incorrectly	Word Study & Vocabulary Kit 1, Units 25–27
39. con<u>qu</u>er 40. mu<u>sc</u>le	Consonants	1 or more items incorrectly	Word Study & Vocabulary Kit 2, Units 21–24
41. <u>pre</u>mix 42. strang<u>ely</u> 43. fu<u>zz</u>ier	Affixes	1 or more items incorrectly	Word Study & Vocabulary Kit 1, Units 28–31
44. <u>ex</u>clude 45. <u>bi</u>ceps 46. <u>fore</u>ground 47. <u>in</u>jury 48. <u>tri</u>angle 49. certain<u>ly</u> 50. <u>non</u>profit	Affixes	1 or more items incorrectly	Word Study & Vocabulary Kit 2, Units 25–29

Initial Screening and Placement Assessment Form B

Word List	Feature	If students answer...	Then provide instruction using...
1. misbehave 2. aftermath 3. demolish 4. submit	Prefixes	1 or more items incorrectly	Word Study & Vocabulary Kit 3, Units 1–4
5. irrigate 6. collide 7. surrender 8. opposite 9. assorted 10. inaccurate	Prefixes	1 or more items incorrectly	Word Study & Vocabulary Kit 4, Units 5–9
11. heavily 12. dimmest 13. musician 14. emptiness 15. grocery 16. difficulty	Suffixes	1 or more items incorrectly	Word Study & Vocabulary Kit 3, Units 5–17
17. evidence 18. occupancy 19. reasonable 20. believable	Suffixes	1 or more items incorrectly	Word Study & Vocabulary Kit 4, Units 1–4
21. assumption 22. gravity 23. volcanic 24. indication 25. majority	Vowel and Consonant Alternations	1 or more items incorrectly	Word Study & Vocabulary Kit 3, Units 18–23

Initial Screening and Placement Assessment Form B *(cont'd)*

Words	Greek and Latin Elements	2 or more items incorrectly	Word Study & Vocabulary Kit
26. <u>uni</u>verse 27. <u>super</u>hero 28. <u>photo</u>graph 29. <u>geo</u>logy 30. in<u>spect</u>or 31. <u>audio</u>	Greek and Latin Elements	2 or more items incorrectly	Word Study & Vocabulary Kit 3, Units 24–29
32. <u>quadr</u>uple 33. <u>equal</u>ity 34. contra<u>dict</u> 35. e<u>rupt</u>ion 36. <u>terr</u>itory 37. epi<u>dem</u>ic 38. <u>demo</u>cracy 39. <u>prim</u>itive 40. <u>tri</u>pod 41. se<u>cur</u>ity 42. <u>patri</u>otic 43. <u>bene</u>fit 44. pro<u>duce</u> 45. <u>gen</u>etic 46. re<u>cept</u>ion 47. <u>cred</u>entials 48. <u>fluct</u>uate 49. <u>bio</u>logical 50. <u>sect</u>ional	Greek and Latin Elements	2 or more items incorrectly	Word Study & Vocabulary Kit 4, Units 10–26

Pre- and Post-Assessments for Feature Analysis

These assessments are additional tools for determining student needs and progress over time. Teachers can select from a variety of assessment options that target a related group of units by similar features (or skills).

Assessment options include:

- **Spelling**
- **Reading**

Choose which assessment form to administer to students. See pages 42–45 for the Master Word Lists.

Assessment	Purpose	Frequency
Form A: Spelling Pre- and Post-Assessment	Identify features for a related set of skills that students can spell correctly before and after instruction.	Before and after teaching a related set of skills (8 times a year)
Form B: Reading Pre- and Post-Assessment	Identify features for a related set of skills that students can read correctly before and after instruction.	Before and after teaching a related set of skills (8 times a year)

Spelling Pre- and Post-Assessments • Form A

Instructions for Administering, Scoring, Analyzing, and Reporting Results

Administer the Spelling Pre- and Post-Assessments

1. Make a copy of the Spelling Pre- and Post-Assessment Student Form A (page 46).

2. Administer the pre- and post-assessment to small groups of students at the same time or to your entire class. Note: Use the same word list for pre- and post-assessment.

3. Explain to students that you will be calling out words one at a time and using each word in a sentence. Students are to write each word on their recording forms.

4. Collect students' recording forms at the end of the assessment.

Score the Spelling Pre- and Post-Assessments

The maximum score is 20 points, 2 points per word.

1. If the entire word is spelled correctly, score it as 2 points.

2. If the word is misspelled but the feature is spelled correctly, score it as 1 point. (See underlined features of each word on the Master Word Lists found on pages 42–45.)

3. If the word and the feature are misspelled, score it as 0 points.

4. Document any errors (misspelled words and/or features).

5. Total the score for the assessment. Record the total score at the bottom of the page.

Analyze Results and Plan for Instruction

1. Analyze the results to determine if the student has mastered the unit skills or needs further instruction, reinforcement, or practice.

2. Look for evidence of transfer in students' reading and writing for application of word study and vocabulary learning.

Pre-Assessment Results

Student Score	Next Steps
18 to 20 points **Enrichment, Independent Level**	Student has control of the unit skills. Provide enrichment and more challenging activities to support continued learning.
14 to 17 points **Moderate Support,** **Instructional Level**	Student has control of many of the unit skills. Provide reinforcement for areas of need through differentiated instruction. Identify specific skills needing additional support. Re-assess to determine mastery or the need for additional interventions.
0 to 13 points **Intervention, Frustrational/** **Challenging Level**	Student is in need of instruction for most of the unit skills. Provide additional reinforcement and intervention lessons to support learning. Re-assess to determine mastery or the need for additional interventions. Continue to provide additional supports and differentiated instruction throughout the unit.

Post-Assessment Results

Student Score	Next Steps
18 to 20 points **Enrichment, Independent Level**	Student has mastered the unit skills. Provide enrichment and more challenging activities to support continued learning. Proceed to the next unit of study.
14 to 17 points **Moderate Support, Instructional Level**	Student has control of many of the unit skills. Provide reinforcement for areas of need. Identify specific skills needing additional support. Re-assess to determine mastery or the need for additional interventions. Proceed to the next unit of study.
0 to 13 points **Intervention, Frustrational/ Challenging Level**	Student is in need of additional instruction of most of the unit skills. Provide additional reinforcement and intervention lessons to support learning. Re-assess to determine mastery or the need for additional interventions. Continue to provide additional supports and differentiated instruction in the next unit of study.

Report Results from the Spelling Pre- and Post-Assessments

1. Use the Pre- and Post-Assessment Class Summary sheets (pages 34–41) to document learning over time. These forms provides a summary of ongoing progress for the class throughout the school year.

2. Use the summary to flexibly group students for appropriate continued learning and intervention.

3. Color code student scores to identify small groups for additional support and intervention.

4. For students who need moderate support, highlight their scores in yellow.

5. For students who need intensive interventions and support, highlight their scores in pink (or red).

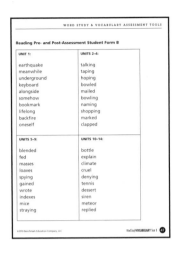

Reading Pre- and Post-Assessments

Instructions for Administering, Scoring, Analyzing, and Reporting Results (Form B)

Administer the Reading Pre- and Post-Assessments

1. Make a copy of Student Recording Form B (page 47–48) and the matching Teacher Recording Form B (pages 49–56).

2. Administer the pre- or post-assessment to individual students. Note: use the same word list for pre- and post-assessments.

3. Explain to students that you will be giving them a list of words to read. As they read the list, you will record if they read each word or parts of each word correctly. You will use what you learned to support their learning in the upcoming lessons.

4. Collect student recording forms at the end of the assessment.

Score the Reading Pre- and Post-Assessments

The maximum score is 20 points, 2 points per word.

1. If the entire word is read correctly, score it as 2 points.

2. If the feature is read correctly, score it as 1 point. Note: the feature may be read correctly even if the entire word is not read correctly. (See underlined features of each word on the Master Word Lists found on pages 42–45.)

3. If the word and the feature are misread, score it as 0 points.

4. Document any errors (mispronounced words and/or features).

5. Total the score for the assessment. Record the total score at the bottom of the page.

Analyze Results and Plan for Instruction

1. Analyze the results to determine if the student has mastered the unit skills or needs further instruction, reinforcement, or practice.

2. Look for evidence of transfer in students' reading and writing for application of word study and vocabulary learning.

Pre-Assessment Results

Student Score	Next Steps
18 to 20 points **Enrichment, Independent Level**	Student has control of the unit skills. Provide enrichment and more challenging activities to support continued learning.
14 to 17 points **Moderate Support, Instructional Level**	Student has control of many of the unit skills. Provide reinforcement for areas of need through differentiated instruction. Identify specific skills needing additional support. Re-assess to determine mastery or the need for additional interventions.
0 to 13 points **Intervention, Frustrational/ Challenging Level**	Student is in need of instruction for most of the unit skills. Provide additional reinforcement and intervention lessons to support learning. Re-assess to determine mastery or the need for additional interventions. Continue to provide additional supports and differentiated instruction throughout the unit.

Post-Assessment Results

Student Score	Next Steps
18 to 20 points **Enrichment, Independent Level**	Student has mastered the unit skills. Provide enrichment and more challenging activities to support continued learning. Proceed to the next unit of study.
14 to 17 points **Moderate Support, Instructional Level**	Student has control of many of the unit skills. Provide reinforcement for areas of need. Identify specific skills needing additional support. Re-assess to determine mastery or the need for additional interventions. Proceed to the next unit of study.
0 to 13 points **Intervention, Frustrational/ Challenging Level**	Student is in need of additional instruction of most of the unit skills. Provide additional reinforcement and intervention lessons to support learning. Re-assess to determine mastery or the need for additional interventions. Continue to provide additional supports and differentiated instruction in the next unit of study.

Report Results from the Reading Pre- and Post-Assessments

1. Use the Pre- and Post-Assessment Class Summary sheets (pages 34–41) to document learning over time. These forms provides a summary of ongoing progress for the class throughout the school year.

2. Use the summary to flexibly group students for appropriate continued learning and intervention.

3. Color code student scores to identify small groups for additional support and intervention. For students who need moderate support, highlight their scores in yellow. For students who need intensive interventions and support, highlight their scores in pink (or red).

Unit 1 Pre- and Post-Assessment Class Summary

Teacher Name: _____ Grade Level: _____

Unit 1: Compound Words				
Student Names	**Spelling Pretest** Date Administered:	**Spelling Posttest** Date Administered:	**Reading Pretest** Date Administered:	**Reading Posttest** Date Administered:

Units 2–4 Pre- and Post-Assessment Class Summary

Teacher Name: _____   Grade Level: _____

	Units 2–4: Inflectional Endings			
	Spelling **Pretest**	**Spelling** **Posttest**	**Reading** **Pretest**	**Reading** **Posttest**
Student Names	Date Administered:	Date Administered:	Date Administered:	Date Administered:

Units 5–9 Pre- and Post-Assessment Class Summary

Teacher Name: _____ Grade Level: _____

| Student Names | Units 5–9: Inflectional Endings | | | |
	Spelling Pretest Date Administered:	Spelling Posttest Date Administered:	Reading Pretest Date Administered:	Reading Posttest Date Administered:

Units 10–14 Pre- and Post-Assessment Class Summary

Teacher Name: _____ Grade Level: _____

Student Names	Units 10–14: Open and Closed Syllables			
	Spelling Pretest Date Administered:	**Spelling Posttest** Date Administered:	**Reading Pretest** Date Administered:	**Reading Posttest** Date Administered:

Units 15–19 Pre- and Post-Assessment Class Summary

Teacher Name: _____ Grade Level: _____

Units 15–19: Vowel Patterns in Accented/Stressed Syllables				
Student Names	**Speiling Pretest** Date Administered:	**Spelling Posttest** Date Administered:	**Reading Pretest** Date Administered:	**Reading Posttest** Date Administered:

Units 20–24 Pre- and Post-Assessment Class Summary

Teacher Name: _____   Grade Level: _____

	Units 20–24: Unaccented Syllables			
Student Names	**Spelling Pretest** Date Administered:	**Spelling Posttest** Date Administered:	**Reading Pretest** Date Administered:	**Reading Posttest** Date Administered:

Units 25–27 Pre- and Post-Assessment Class Summary

Teacher Name: _____ Grade Level: _____

Units 25–27: Consonants				
Student Names	**Spelling Pretest** Date Administered:	**Spelling Posttest** Date Administered:	**Reading Pretest** Date Administered:	**Reading Posttest** Date Administered:

Units 28–31 Pre- and Post-Assessment Class Summary

Teacher Name: _____ Grade Level: _____

Units 28–31: Affixes				
	Spelling Pretest	**Spelling Posttest**	**Reading Pretest**	**Reading Posttest**
Student Names	Date Administered:	Date Administered:	Date Administered:	Date Administered:

Pre- and Post-Assessments

Master Word Lists for Feature Analysis
Unit 1: Compound Words

Unit 1 Form A (Spelling Pre- and Post-Assessment)	
1. airplane	6. become
2. handmade	7. schoolhouse
3. sunlight	8. eyeball
4. seashore	9. upstream
5. footprint	10. uplift

Unit 1 Form B (Reading Pre- and Post-Assessment)	
1. earthquake	6. somehow
2. meanwhile	7. bookmark
3. underground	8. lifelong
4. keyboard	9. backfire
5. alongside	10. oneself

Units 2–4: Inflectional Endings

Units 2–4 Form A (Spelling Pre- and Post-Assessment)	
1. asking	6. melting
2. making	7. piling
3. chaining	8. pouting
4. shopped	9. wrecked
5. named	10. hoped

Units 2–4 Form B (Reading Pre- and Post-Assessment)	
1. talking	6. bowling
2. taping	7. naming
3. hoping	8. shopping
4. bowled	9. marked
5. mailed	10. clapped

Master Word Lists for Feature Analysis *(cont'd)*

Units 5–9: Inflectional Endings

Units 5–9 Form A (Spelling Pre- and Post-Assessment)

1. sta<u>red</u>	6. trot<u>ted</u>
2. <u>knew</u>	7. <u>said</u>
3. pebbl<u>es</u>	8. pea<u>ches</u>
4. oursel<u>ves</u>	9. <u>children</u>
5. play<u>ing</u>	10. spray<u>ing</u>

Units 5–9 Form B (Reading Pre- and Post-Assessment)

1. blen<u>ded</u>	6. gai<u>ned</u>
2. <u>fed</u>	7. <u>wrote</u>
3. mas<u>ses</u>	8. inde<u>xes</u>
4. loa<u>ves</u>	9. <u>mice</u>
5. sp<u>ying</u>	10. stra<u>ying</u>

Units 10–14: Open and Closed Syllables

Units 10–14 Form A (Spelling Pre- and Post-Assessment)

1. <u>con</u>tact	6. <u>mus</u>tard
2. <u>ro</u>dent	7. <u>fin</u>ish
3. <u>mo</u>ment	8. <u>va</u>cant
4. <u>cre</u>ate	9. <u>du</u>et
5. <u>hop</u>ped	10. <u>plot</u>ted

Units 10–14 Form B (Reading Pre- and Post-Assessment)

1. <u>bot</u>tle	6. <u>ten</u>nis
2. <u>ex</u>plain	7. <u>des</u>sert
3. <u>cli</u>mate	8. <u>si</u>ren
4. <u>cru</u>el	9. <u>me</u>teor
5. <u>de</u>nying	10. <u>re</u>plied

Master Word Lists for Feature Analysis *(cont'd)*

Units 15–19: Vowel Patterns in Accented/Stressed Syllables

Units 15–19 Form A (Spelling Pre- and Post-Assessment)	
1. rainbow	6. failure
2. decide	7. sidewalk
3. cobra	8. notice
4. jukebox	9. amuse
5. female	10. veto

Units 15–19 Form B (Reading Pre- and Post-Assessment)	
1. crater	6. vapor
2. tighten	7. brightness
3. lonesome	8. soapy
4. tubeless	9. bugle
5. ceiling	10. neither

Units 20–24: Unaccented Syllables

Units 20–24 Form A (Spelling Pre- and Post-Assessment)	
1. trample	6. freckle
2. central	7. fender
3. solar	8. speaker
4. beggar	9. treaty
5. empty	10. global

Units 20–24 Form B (Reading Pre- and Post-Assessment)	
1. needle	6. scribble
2. fossil	7. council
3. terror	8. stellar
4. vendor	9. burglar
5. chimney	10. trolley

Master Word Lists for Feature Analysis *(cont'd)*

Units 25–27: Consonants

Units 25–27 Form A (Spelling Pre- and Post-Assessment)	
1. cubic	6. civic
2. gesture	7. genius
3. network	8. attack
4. remind	9. retake
5. untie	10. undone

Units 25–27 Form B (Reading Pre- and Post-Assessment)	
1. atomic	6. elastic
2. ginger	7. gopher
3. potluck	8. panic
4. reclaim	9. rewind
5. unable	10. unsure

Units 28–31: Affixes

Units 28–31 Form A (Spelling Pre- and Post-Assessment)	
1. disagree	6. distaste
2. mislead	7. misuse
3. filthy	8. worthy
4. eagerly	9. heavily
5. toughest	10. lazier

Units 28–31 Form B (Reading Pre- and Post-Assessment)	
1. premix	6. pregame
2. dismissed	7. misplace
3. mistrust	8. strangely
4. directly	9. sincerely
5. dimmest	10. fuzzier

Spelling Pre- and Post-Assessment Student Form A

Name: _____   Date: _____

☐ Pretest   ☐ Posttest

_____ Total # Words Read Correctly   _____ Total # Features Read Correctly   _____ Total Combined Score

Instructions: In the spaces below, record each word your teacher provides you.	Correctly Spelled Word (2 points)	Correctly Spelled Feature (1 point)	Incorrectly Spelled Word & Feature (0 points)
1.			
2.			
3.			
4.			
5.			
6.			
7.			
8.			
9.			
10.			
Total Points (20 possible)			

Reading Pre- and Post-Assessment Student Form B

UNIT 1:	UNITS 2–4:
earthquake	talking
meanwhile	taping
underground	hoping
keyboard	bowled
alongside	mailed
somehow	bowling
bookmark	naming
lifelong	shopping
backfire	marked
oneself	clapped
UNITS 5–9:	**UNITS 10–14:**
blended	bottle
fed	explain
masses	climate
loaves	cruel
spying	denying
gained	tennis
wrote	dessert
indexes	siren
mice	meteor
straying	replied

Reading Pre- and Post-Assessment Student Form B *(cont'd)*

UNITS 15–19:	UNITS 20–24:
crater	needle
tighten	fossil
lonesome	terror
tubeless	vendor
ceiling	chimney
vapor	scribble
brightness	council
soapy	stellar
bugle	burglar
neither	trolley

UNITS 25–27:	UNITS 28–31:
atomic	premix
ginger	dismissed
potluck	mistrust
reclaim	directly
unable	dimmest
elastic	pregame
gopher	misplace
panic	strangely
rewind	sincerely
unsure	fuzzier

Reading Pre- and Post-Assessment Teacher Recording Form B

Unit 1: Compound Words

Name: _____   Date: _____

☐ Pretest   ☐ Posttest

_____ Total # Words Read Correctly   _____ Total # Features Read Correctly   _____ Total Combined Score

Instructions: As students read each word from the unit list, place a check mark in the appropriate column noting how they read each word or feature.	Correctly Read Word (2 points)	Incorrectly Read Word/Correctly Read Feature (1 point)	Incorrectly Read Word & Feature (0 points)
1. earthquake			
2. meanwhile			
3. underground			
4. keyboard			
5. alongside			
6. somehow			
7. bookmark			
8. lifelong			
9. backfire			
10. oneself			
Total Points (20 possible)			

Reading Pre- and Post-Assessment Teacher Recording Form B

Units 2–4: Inflectional Endings

Name: _____   Date: _____

☐ Pretest   ☐ Posttest

_____ Total # Words Read Correctly   _____ Total # Features Read Correctly   _____ Total Combined Score

Instructions: As students read each word from the unit list, place a check mark in the appropriate column noting how they read each word or feature.	Correctly Read Word (2 points)	Incorrectly Read Word/Correctly Read Feature (1 point)	Incorrectly Read Word & Feature (0 points)
1. tal<u>king</u>			
2. ta<u>ping</u>			
3. ho<u>ping</u>			
4. bow<u>led</u>			
5. mai<u>led</u>			
6. bow<u>ling</u>			
7. na<u>ming</u>			
8. sho<u>pping</u>			
9. mar<u>ked</u>			
10. clap<u>ped</u>			
Total Points (20 possible)			

Reading Pre- and Post-Assessment Teacher Recording Form B

Units 5–9: Inflectional Endings

Name: _____ Date: _____

☐ Pretest   ☐ Posttest

_____ Total # Words Read Correctly   _____ Total # Features Read Correctly   _____ Total Combined Score

Instructions: As students read each word from the unit list, place a check mark in the appropriate column noting how they read each word or feature.	Correctly Read Word (2 points)	Incorrectly Read Word/Correctly Read Feature (1 point)	Incorrectly Read Word & Feature (0 points)
1. blen<u>ded</u>			
2. <u>fed</u>			
3. mas<u>ses</u>			
4. loa<u>ves</u>			
5. spy<u>ing</u>			
6. gai<u>ned</u>			
7. <u>wrote</u>			
8. inde<u>xes</u>			
9. <u>mice</u>			
10. stray<u>ing</u>			
Total Points (20 possible)			

Reading Pre- and Post-Assessment Teacher Recording Form B

Units 10–14: Open and Closed Syllables

Name: _____ Date: _____

☐ Pretest   ☐ Posttest

_____ Total # Words Read Correctly   _____ Total # Features Read Correctly   _____ Total Combined Score

Instructions: As students read each word from the unit list, place a check mark in the appropriate column noting how they read each word or feature.	Correctly Read Word (2 points)	Incorrectly Read Word/Correctly Read Feature (1 point)	Incorrectly Read Word & Feature (0 points)
1. bottle			
2. explain			
3. climate			
4. cruel			
5. denying			
6. tennis			
7. dessert			
8. siren			
9. meteor			
10. replied			
Total Points (20 possible)			

Reading Pre- and Post-Assessment Teacher Recording Form B

Units 15–19: Vowel Patterns in Accented/Stressed Syllables

Name: _____   Date: _____

☐ Pretest   ☐ Posttest

_____ Total # Words Read Correctly   _____ Total # Features Read Correctly   _____ Total Combined Score

Instructions: As students read each word from the unit list, place a check mark in the appropriate column noting how they read each word or feature.	Correctly Read Word (2 points)	Incorrectly Read Word/Correctly Read Feature (1 point)	Incorrectly Read Word & Feature (0 points)
1. cr<u>a</u>ter			
2. t<u>i</u>ghten			
3. <u>lone</u>some			
4. <u>tube</u>less			
5. c<u>ei</u>ling			
6. <u>va</u>por			
7. br<u>i</u>ghtness			
8. s<u>oa</u>py			
9. b<u>u</u>gle			
10. n<u>ei</u>ther			
Total Points (20 possible)			

Reading Pre- and Post-Assessment Teacher Recording Form B

Units 20–24: Unaccented Syllables

Name: _____   Date: _____

☐ Pretest   ☐ Posttest

_____ Total # Words Read Correctly   _____ Total # Features Read Correctly   _____ Total Combined Score

Instructions: As students read each word from the unit list, place a check mark in the appropriate column noting how they read each word or feature.	Correctly Read Word (2 points)	Incorrectly Read Word/Correctly Read Feature (1 point)	Incorrectly Read Word & Feature (0 points)
1. needle			
2. fossil			
3. terror			
4. vendor			
5. chimney			
6. scribble			
7. council			
8. stellar			
9. burglar			
10. trolley			
Total Points (20 possible)			

Reading Pre- and Post-Assessment Teacher Recording Form B

Units 25–27: Consonants

Name: _____ Date: _____

☐ Pretest   ☐ Posttest

_____ Total # Words Read Correctly   _____ Total # Features Read Correctly   _____ Total Combined Score

Instructions: As students read each word from the unit list, place a check mark in the appropriate column noting how they read each word or feature.	Correctly Read Word (2 points)	Incorrectly Read Word/Correctly Read Feature (1 point)	Incorrectly Read Word & Feature (0 points)
1. atom<u>ic</u>			
2. <u>g</u>inger			
3. potlu<u>ck</u>			
4. <u>re</u>claim			
5. <u>un</u>able			
6. elast<u>ic</u>			
7. <u>g</u>opher			
8. pan<u>ic</u>			
9. <u>re</u>wind			
10. <u>un</u>sure			
Total Points (20 possible)			

Reading Pre- and Post-Assessment Teacher Recording Form B

Units 28–31: Affixes

Name: _____ Date: _____

☐ Pretest ☐ Posttest

_____ Total # Words Read Correctly _____ Total # Features Read Correctly _____ Total Combined Score

Instructions: As students read each word from the unit list, place a check mark in the appropriate column noting how they read each word or feature.	Correctly Read Word (2 points)	Incorrectly Read Word/Correctly Read Feature (1 point)	Incorrectly Read Word & Feature (0 points)
1. premix			
2. dismissed			
3. mistrust			
4. directly			
5. dimmest			
6. pregame			
7. misplace			
8. strangely			
9. sincerely			
10. fuzzier			
Total Points (20 possible)			

Unit Quick-Check Assessments

Unit Quick-Check Assessments provide unit-specific assessments to determine mastery and student needs on a weekly basis. Quick-Check Assessments can be used to form flexible groups in need of enrichment or intervention. These assessment tools provide ongoing progress monitoring for documenting student growth and learning over time.

Instructions for Administering, Scoring, Analyzing, and Reporting Results

Administer and Score the Unit Quick-Check Assessment

1. Make a copy of the student Quick-Check Assessment found on page 8 of the Teacher's Guide for each unit.

2. Administer the Quick-Check Assessments to students after completing each unit.

3. Score the correct responses and total the number correct out of the possible score for each Unit Quick-Check.

Analyze Results and Plan for Instruction

1. Analyze the results to determine if the student has mastered the unit skills or needs further instruction, reinforcement, or practice.

2. Look for evidence of transfer in students' reading and writing for application of word study and vocabulary learning.

Student Score	Next Steps
Enrichment 90–100%	Student has mastered the unit skills. Provide enrichment and more challenging activities to support continued learning. Proceed to the next unit of study.
Moderate Support 70–89%	Student has control of many of the unit skills. Provide reinforcement for areas of need. Identify specific skills needing additional support. Re-assess to determine mastery or the need for additional interventions. Proceed to the next unit of study.
Intervention 0–69%	Student is in need of additional instruction of most of the unit skills. Provide additional reinforcement and intervention lessons to support learning. Re-assess to determine mastery or the need for additional interventions. Continue to provide additional supports and differentiated instruction in the next unit of study.

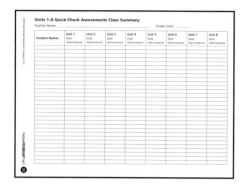

Reporting Results from the Quick-Check Assessment

1. Use the Unit Quick-Check Assessments Class Summary sheets (pages 59–62) to document learning over time. These forms provide a summary of ongoing progress for the class throughout the school year.

2. Use the summary to flexibly group students for appropriate continued learning and intervention.

3. Color code student scores to identify small groups for additional support and intervention. For students who need moderate support, highlight their scores in yellow. For students who need intensive interventions and support, highlight their scores in pink (or red).

Units 1–8 Quick-Check Assessments Class Summary

Teacher Name: _____

Grade Level: _____

Student Names	Unit 1 Date Administered:	Unit 2 Date Administered:	Unit 3 Date Administered:	Unit 4 Date Administered:	Unit 5 Date Administered:	Unit 6 Date Administered:	Unit 7 Date Administered:	Unit 8 Date Administered:

Units 9–16 Quick-Check Assessments Class Summary

Teacher Name: _____

Grade Level: _____

Student Names	Unit 9 Date Administered:	Unit 10 Date Administered:	Unit 11 Date Administered:	Unit 12 Date Administered:	Unit 13 Date Administered:	Unit 14 Date Administered:	Unit 15 Date Administered:	Unit 16 Date Administered:

Units 17–24 Quick-Check Assessments Class Summary

Teacher Name: _____   Grade Level: _____

Student Names	Unit 17 Date Administered:	Unit 18 Date Administered:	Unit 19 Date Administered:	Unit 20 Date Administered:	Unit 21 Date Administered:	Unit 22 Date Administered:	Unit 23 Date Administered:	Unit 24 Date Administered:

Units 25–32 Quick-Check Assessments Class Summary

Teacher Name: _____ Grade Level: _____

Student Names	Unit 25 Date Administered:	Unit 26 Date Administered:	Unit 27 Date Administered:	Unit 28 Date Administered:	Unit 29 Date Administered:	Unit 30 Date Administered:	Unit 31 Date Administered:	Unit 32 Date Administered:

Dear Parent/Guardian,

This year your child will participate in the Word Study & Vocabulary program from Benchmark Education Company. Although word study is only one of the many daily literacy activities in our classroom, this instruction provides students with a valuable tool in the complex task of learning to read, comprehend, and enjoy a variety of texts.

In Word Study & Vocabulary lessons, students learn strategies for decoding, spelling, and understanding the meaning of multisyllabic words. Every week we'll review and practice previously taught skills and explore important new ones. Students will also participate in frequent, brief assessments in spelling, word meaning, and word analysis so that we can immediately address learning needs. You have an important role in this process as well. Watch for a *Home Connection* activity each week, and please continue to read to and with your child each day.

I look forward to an exciting year of learning, and I thank you for your help as your child learns to read longer and more difficult texts. Don't hesitate to contact me with any questions or concerns.

Sincerely,

Estimado(a) señor(a):

Durante el transcurso de este año su hijo participará en el programa de vocabulario y el estudio de palabras de Benchmark Education Company. Aunque el estudio de palabras es sólo una de las actividades cotidianas en nuestra aula, esta destreza sirve como una herramienta clave en la tarea compleja de formar a un lector comprensivo que disfrute de una variedad de textos.

En las lecciones de estudio de palabras y de vocabulario, el estudiante aprende a descodificar las palabras, a deletrear con confianza y a comprender el significado de palabras difíciles. Cada semana repasaremos destrezas de la semana anterior y aprenderemos destrezas nuevas. También el estudiante participará en evaluaciones breves y frecuentes de ortografía, significado y análisis de palabras para que podamos remediar cualquier duda en su momento. Usted tendrá un papel importante en este proceso. Usted recibirá una *actividad de Participación de los padres* cada semana y, por favor, siga leyendo con su hijo a diario.

Anticipo un año emocionante de aprendizaje y quisiera agradecérselo a usted de antemano, el papel integral que desempeñará en ayudar a su hijo a aprender a leer textos cada vez más complejos. Me despido de usted cordialmente y le reitero que estoy a sus órdenes para cualquier aclaración o duda.

Atentamente